Darkroom Photography

The Complete Guide to Mastering the Basics of Darkroom Photography

James Carren

Table of Contents

Introduction

Analog photography is a dying art. When I was in art school and first told that I'd have to take a film photography class, I scoffed. What was the use, I thought, when the entire industry is digital now? Little did I know that some of the most specialized and high-paying jobs that exist are those of people who have the skills to develop film and make darkroom prints. Not only that, but I found that, despite the expense and the hard work required, darkroom was my favorite way to make a photograph.

Darkroom is a science and an art, and it engages your mind in such a way that sitting in front of a computer screen never will, because you get to use your hands and actually watch the chemistry react, watch the image appear right before your eyes. There is something so unique and sacred about that to me.

While this book is mainly meant for those that have never encountered darkroom before and would like to learn the skills, I hope that somewhere in these tips a seasoned photographer might find an alternate way of doing things or an idea that serves them well.

I want to walk through the entire process with you, and give you ideas of how to have resources such as a darkroom where perhaps you currently have none. God knows I've been there.

I'll start from the very beginning: how to select your film and expose it correctly, how to open a film canister, develop the film, and make prints. Then I'll explain how to finish prints and scan the film for digital use, because I feel that it's important to have both versions available to you. I've even included a section on two different types of toners so that you can make your prints stand out just a little bit more.

My goal is to open up the world of film to my generation, so that it continues in its long tradition.

A Quick Rundown on Shooting Film

Shooting film is a little bit different from shooting digital, although if you already have a good, solid foundation, then the principles remain the same. In fact, I have found that most people begin to become great photographers after they have had some experience in the darkroom. The reason for this lies in the fact that analog photography is a much more hands-on process that doesn't provide instant gratification. Therefore, you can't just look at a photograph on a monitor and say, "Oh well that's too bright, let me shoot it again." You have to have a pretty good idea of what you're doing from the start.

Since this book focuses on black and white photography, I would suggest sticking with that. In some respects, color is easier because it's now such a specialized niche that you have to send it off to get it developed. But you also have to make prints digitally, and that's not what this book focuses on.

There are many, many brands of film you can choose from, and it's all up to personal preference. They all perform in generally the same way, but since each film is made by a slightly different process, some are richer than others, some develop more nicely, and some are easier to open. I initially learned on Kodak Tri-X film, but I find it a bit dull in richness and hard to open. I much prefer Kodak T-Max and Ilford Delta. You're never going to know what you like until you shoot it though, so I would suggest creating a little sample pack for yourself to try things out.

ISO also changes things. ISO refers to the speed of your film, or how sensitive to light it is. You probably already know from your digital camera that when you have your ISO set low, like 100 or 200, the sensor lets in a lot less light than if you have it set to 1600. You might also have noticed that pictures taken at low ISOs are much smoother, meaning they have less grain or noise. ISO is all up to a combination of personal preference and light conditions; high ISO is more suitable in low light situations, but you still need to adjust your exposure accordingly. If you are a beginner, or even if you just don't know what you need, start around 400 ISO. It's right smack in the middle of the spectrum and should provide you with good highlights and shadows within a decent spectrum of light.

You'll also have to be meticulous to figure out the correct exposures for things. Try to find nice even light to practice in for your first few rolls, it'll give you a good baseline. Remember that exposure is made up of ISO, aperture, and shutter speed. Shutter speed controls how much movement you see in an image, and aperture controls depth of field, which is how far back you can see into an image.

Also remember that, with film as with digital, if you focus on an area of extreme brightness, your photo will underexpose to compensate and vice versa. To avoid that on your film, you should focus on an area of middle grey to take your reading, then take the photo. It also might be a good idea to try bracketing, which is where you take a photo at the exposure you believe it should be, then close down one stop, and then a second stop, and take a shot at both. You can also do the same going up the scale, although I find that with film, stopping down one or two stops is usually sufficient.

From there, you're ready to go out and shoot.

Prepping Film For Development

After you've shot your film, it's almost time to develop. But if you're working with either 35mm or 120mm, you first have to rewind your film. First, it's important to determine whether or not you have a manual rewind or an automatic rewind. If you have a manual rewind, there will most likely be a crank on top of the camera. Pay attention to the numbers on your camera as you shoot, and keep in mind whether you're shooting a 24 exposure roll or 36 exposure roll. On some rolls of film, you might be able to get more than the expected amount of exposures. This is perfectly okay, but can pose a problem when it comes to storage of negatives. Once you finish your roll of film, you should be able to feel the tension in the camera release a little bit. This means that you've reached the end of your roll of film.

Before you rewind, you should check out your camera's manual and see if there are any special instructions when it comes to rewinding the film. On some cameras, there is a latch at the bottom of the camera that you have to release in order to begin the rewinding process. This is put in place so that you don't accidentally begin to rewind your film as you're shooting. If it's there, release the latch, and begin to wind. You should be able to feel and hear the click of each sprocket as the film is rewound, and the pressure will feel different as you reach the end. Once that pressure releases, it is safe to open the back of your camera. Don't worry if there is a little bit of a film tail sticking out from the canister. If you've rewound it enough, this should just be the end of the film, not an actual exposure, and having the tail sticking out can actually make it easier to get the film out of the canister later.

By nature, an automatic rewind should begin doing its job as soon as you have reached the end of your film. If it doesn't, and you get a few extra exposures, that's no big deal. However, if you don't want these extra exposures, you can check the bottom of your camera to see if there is a recessed button on the bottom. If so, you can use the tip of the pen or pencil to press it and start rewind. Typically, automatic rewind works extremely well, but I did have an instance once where my camera was very old and so the mechanism had broken, causing rewind to stop with about ten exposures to go. If this happens, you might actually be able to hear it, because in the case of my camera, you can hear the motor, and it had begun to sound weak and even stop entirely. Stupid me, I still opened the back of the camera in the light to see what was happening. I would suggest that if you think this might ever be the case with your camera, you take it into a film changing closet or a darkroom before opening the back.

After you're finished rewinding film, it's time to load it onto reels. Pay attention to whether you have 35 or 120mm, because you need a different sized reel for each. And if you happen to have film that is a weird in-between size, be aware that you might have to take a used reel from a roll of film that's already been developed and cut it down so you have something to load it onto.

That aside, I'm going to focus the rest of this chapter and the development chapter using the assumption of 35mm. There are a few things you're going to need in order to load your film and they are: a loading tank, reels, a can opener, and scissors, as well as a loading room or a film change bag. The trick with loading film is that you have to learn to do it by feel because the film cannot be exposed to light or it will be completely ruined (and if even a little light gets in under the door or into the bag, you'll have light leaks or fog on your film, which is fixable in Photoshop, but then you can't make a darkroom print). In order to learn how to do it by feel, I would suggest sacrificing a roll of blank or leaked film to practice on.

You'll also need to decide what kind of reels you'd like to use; there are traditional metal ones and plastic ones. Both work the same, it's just all up to personal preference. I find the plastic ones easier to work with. On your reel, you'll notice two guides, which can either be rectangular or triangular in shape. This is what gets your film onto the track, and you're going to guide your film under them, however, there is a trick to it. We'll get to that in a minute.

You should also decide what kind of tank you want to use. There are myriad brands, but the two I have experience with are Paterson and Jobo. Both are great, but I prefer the Paterson because the water drains out much easier during the rinsing process.

When you're ready to open your film, you'll need to lay out all your things before you shut the door, and put them in an order where you can find everything. You should take the tank apart and set aside the rod, funnel and top. Just a note too . . . even if you're only developing only one roll of film, you should use the correct amount of reels for the tank. It helps with the weight and with making sure you don't get too much developer saturated in the one roll.

After you've shut the door, the first thing you're going to do is open your film canister. Now, this is going to be really easy if you happened to leave some of the tail sticking out. In that case, all you have to do is pull to get it out of the canister, cut the reel, and load it onto the reel. But if you don't have the tail sticking out then you get to experience the joy of using the can opener to get your film out.

There's no right way to do it; you can open it from the top or from the side with the felt-lined lip. You can also use whichever side of the can opener you prefer, although I find that the sharp end works best to fit under either lip. Different brands of film are actually harder to open than others, so just be patient with yourself and realize it'll take some trial and error. You just have to get enough leverage to pop the top off. Even if you just get it up enough to slip the film out, that's good. Just don't scratch the film.

After you've got it out of the canister, put your thumb against the attached reel and trim the tail off straight. Also trim the other end, but don't cut too much; you don't want to get into your frames.

To load the film onto the reel, make sure that the guides are facing up and pointing towards your body. Guide the end of the film under the lip, and begin to twist the wheel. Just as with film rewinding, you should be able to feel the film going onto the reel. Keep your fingers on either side as extra guides to make sure the film doesn't pop the track, which it will most likely do the first few times you try this. If you continue to try to roll it after it's popped the track, it'll either fall off onto the floor or will create what's referred to as a kiss, where the film touches itself and leaves a mark.

After you've successfully got the film on the roll, it's time to load your tank. Assuming you're working with a two-reeler, put the rod in the middle of the tank and slide your reels down onto it. Never develop without a rod; this can cause light leaks. Never develop with fewer reels than the tank calls for either; the amount of solution will oversaturate the one roll of film. Put your funnel in and screw it on tight. Before putting the top on and opening the door, turn your tank upside down and shake it to ensure that everything is firmly in place. The last thing you want is your film coming out of the tank before it's fully developed. Now, you're ready to develop.

Processing Film For 35mm and 120mm

To develop 35mm and 120mm film, the process is essentially the same, the only difference will be the type of reels used and the amount of chemistry needed. (It's going to vary dependent on whether you have a 2, 3, or 5 reel tank. Setting up the chemistry is very simple; all you have to do is follow the manufacturer's instructions on the back of the package. Just be very careful when buying your supplies and take note that there is a difference between paper and film chemicals. However, if you want to make a print later, you're going to need both.

I prefer Sprint chemistry because I know it works well with lots of types of paper and film and is, generally speaking, hypoallergenic. Keep in mind that if you choose to use a different brand of chemicals, they might not work well with certain types of paper or film. For example, I have found that Kodak paper developer does not jive well with Ilford paper.

So, what do you need to develop your film, which is the first step on the way to making a print?

You will need:

- Developer
- Stop bath
- Fixer
- Fix remover
- Photo flo

- Access to a sink/running water. Make sure that the water you're using is between 68–72 degrees Fahrenheit. I prefer 68. The cooler the water, the slower the development time, which is good for the film.

To develop your film:

- Mix your developer at a 1:9 ratio with water. (You want more water than developer, make sure you don't get it backwards).

- Get out your other chemicals. Use large beakers and fill them up.

- Start with a one minute pre-rinse of just water on the film. Remember to keep your water between 68–72 degrees. Tap your tank on the sink to remove any existing air bubbles.

- For your developer, start counting the second you pour the chemicals into the tank. Use the instructions based on film type. For example, you might only have to develop for five minutes, or it might be 12, depending on developer and film interaction. Agitate for the first 30 seconds, then for 10 seconds of every minute of development. Agitation ensures that the chemicals are flowing around all of the film, and that the chemicals don't become exhausted.

- As soon as your development time is close to up, start pouring the developer down the sink. Note that developer and photo flo can be safely poured down the drain, but everything else needs to either be stored or disposed of in its own container, which can later be taken away by the proper services.

- Pour in your stop bath. Stop time is a minute and a half. Agitate for the first 30 seconds, as before, and tap to remove air bubbles. Agitate every ten seconds of the remaining minute.

- Next comes fixer for 5 minutes. Agitate as before: constantly for the first 30 seconds then ten seconds of every minute.

- A water rinse is next, to remove the remaining fixer from the film. Fill and dump with clean water 15 times.

- Fix remover comes after the water, for one minute. Agitate every ten seconds

- Do another water rinse, this time 30 repetitions.

- You can now take the funnel out of your tank, pour in photo flo, and spin your reels gently for 15–30 seconds. Dump this, and your film is ready to come off the reel and go into the drying cabinet.

- Some people like to completely take their reels apart to remove the film, although if you just pull gently, you should be fine.

- Leave in the drying cabinet at least half an hour.

- If you don't have access to a drying cabinet, you can also dry your film in a dry shower stall, as this is the cleanest, most dust-free area of the house.

Making Contact Sheets

Here's the materials you're going to need to make a print:

- A pack of RC paper

- A pack of fiber paper

- A contact frame

- A mini site

- An adjustable printing easel

- The correct lens for your film format

- A speed easel

- Some cardboard or an empty paper bag

- Graduated filters

- Canned air

After your film is completely dry, it's time to make contact sheets. Rather than wasting precious fiber paper on contact sheets (because you have to use fiber paper for test strips, which I will explain in a minute) you should use RC paper, or resin coated paper. Resin coated paper is very cheap and slick and is by no means archival, so it shouldn't be used for any final product. However, it is good for just seeing what you have on a film strip.

To make your first contact sheet, you should pick out a roll of film. There's no need to take the negatives out of the sleeve. In fact, if you only have a 24 exposure roll, you'll be able to read the title of the sleeve. Now you have to figure out what exposure the contact sheet needs to be at. Using a piece of cardboard, thick paper, or an empty photo paper bag (the black plastic slip) cover up all but the first strip. This is, of course, after you've got your film properly situated on your paper in the exposure frame. Select a good f/stop, not too large or small. F/11 or 16 is usually best. Expose the first strip for 3 seconds. Move your cover down and expose for 6, and so on until you reach the end of the page.

Now you're going to develop the page. As I said before, I use Sprint chemistry. No matter what chemistry you use, you need to check the manufacturer's instructions for how long to develop, stop, and fix. With Sprint, it's two minutes in developer, 15 seconds in stop, and one minute in fix. Make sure you don't rush through this part . . . it may just be a contact sheet test strip, but you want to make sure it's accurate so that you can determine which photos would be the best to try printing.

After you've developed your test strip, take it out into the light and determine what time you need to expose the contact sheet for. The exposure is correct when you can just barely see the sprockets around the image. You can now go make a contact sheet. Now, even if you shot everything on the same day with the same kind of film, you need to repeat this process for every contact sheet. Run your sheets through the paper dryer, or allow them to air-dry.

Next you want to take your contact sheets and look through them for the great photos. If you are a beginner at darkroom, you need to select photos that have a fairly good tonal range, meaning, good detail in the blacks and highlights that aren't blown out. Later, I'll explain how to fix problems like this, but to make your life easier, it's better to pick a really solidly exposed photo for your first print.

I also like to take my contact sheets in the darkroom to help me out, so mark the photos you want to make with a marker for easy reference.

Making A Basic Print

Don't fall under the misconception that whatever the time for your contact sheet was is the time for your photo. You're going to print final images on glossy fiber paper, for one, which reacts differently, and every photo is also different. Make sure your aperture is set to either f/11 or 16, and put your first negative in the holder. In order to make a good test strip and print, you're going to need to make sure it's in focus. For this, you're going to need your mini site and a sheet of fiber paper. You may want to label the back of this paper with FOCUS SHEET so that you don't accidentally try to print on it. Slide this paper into the speed easel or the adjustable easel, whichever you are using. If you're using an adjustable easel, then you need to adjust the blades to hold your paper and then tape them into place. Also, adjustable easels are much heavier than speed easels so they don't move as much. If you're using a speed easel, you may want to tape the sides down to your workspace.

Slide your focus sheet into place, and put your negative into the negative holder. You have to take it out of the sleeve for this, and it's always a good idea to spray it and the negative carrier off with some canned air first to eliminate dust. You might find that this is tricky the first couple of times, and you might have to fiddle around so you don't have any borders around your image. Next, you need to open your stage and slide the negative carrier into place. The silver knobbies face down and hook into the stage to keep it in place. You should be able to feel it latch if it's properly in place.

Turn on your focus light (without the timer; it should stay on until you turn it off) and adjust the height of the lens up or down until you have your photo at the approximate size you want. Make sure your aperture is open to 2.8 to help you focus, but make sure to adjust it back to a reasonable f/16 or 11 before you begin making test strips or you'll be extremely confused. Eyeball it to get it pretty close to sharp, and then pull out your mini site. Place the magnifier over an area where silver is concentrated (a black part of the image) and look through it. If your photo is in focus, then you should be able to see individual grains. If they look swollen or fuzzy, you need to do some tweaking. You want to do this part without the use of a filter.

After everything's in focus, slide your 2 filter over your negative. You want to make sure it's positioned correctly, otherwise it won't be covering the entirety of the print. Now, you're going to find an area of your photo that has a good tonal range exemplary of the photo as a whole. That's the section where you'll expose your test strip. Turn off your light and cut another piece of fiber paper into at least 5–6 strips. Now, you're going to lay that strip on the part you want, and expose for 3 seconds. Expose the second strip for 6, and so on, then develop them the same way as you did your contact sheet. Take it out into the light, and decide which exposure is the best. This is the exposure you'll use for your basic print.

Now, you're going to expose a whole sheet of paper. Keep in mind that you might want to raise or lower your filter to raise or lower the contrast of the image; 2 is just a starting point.

Seems easy right? But that basic print may not be perfect, and you may have to do it over and over to get the filter and the borders just right. Next, I'm going to teach you some techniques to really make your photo pop.

Dodging, Burning and Other Techniques

After you've made a basic print that you're happy with, take a look at it. Even if the exposure is perfect, does it look exactly how you want it to aesthetically? I'm willing to bet that the answer is probably no. Now you need to figure out what areas of the photograph either need to be lighter or darker. You might be thinking, how do I do this without affecting the entire photograph? This is where the advanced techniques of dodging and burning come into play. Dodging is a technique where you make an area of the photograph look lighter than the original, and burning is where you make an area of the photograph look darker. Typically, you want to do this to make your shadows darker or your highlights pop. Let's start with dodging. Let's say you've figured out that your print needs to be exposed at an f/stop of 8, and an exposure time of 12 seconds, but there's an area of the photo that needs to be considerably lighter. You would take either a piece of cardboard, or a piece of dark plastic, and place it over the area that needs to be lightened. You would then expose your photograph for the amount of time, while keeping the lightening area covered. Now the trick is, you also have to figure out how long that area needs to be covered for. Because it's very unlikely that it needs to be covered for the entirety of that 12 seconds. You'll have to do a test strip for this part as well. Let's say you find that the area needs to be covered for three seconds. You would set your timer for 12 seconds, and cover the area for the first three seconds of that exposure. If you just let your cover lay over the area, you will end up with a very awkward line where you can tell that you tried to dodge. In order to avoid this, you have to constantly move your cover during that three seconds of exposure. These techniques are really hard work, so it will take time to get it right.

Burning works in generally the same way, however, you do your exposure and then you add the amount of time you think the area needs. So in that case, you will expose your image for the full 12 seconds and then add however much time you think you need, covering the rest of the image. Again, it will take some experimentation and test strips to figure out that time, and you have to keep your cover moving to avoid unwanted lines.

It's also entirely possible that you will have both dodging and burning that needs to be done on the same image, so you will have to figure out what order to do it in, and your "dance" (the moving of the cover) for each separate photo.

Aside from traditional dodging and burning, you can also use objects of different shapes directly on top of the paper, to add a collage like element to your work. These are called photograms, and they create an outline of the object on top of whatever image you choose. They can also be an image in their own right.

Toning

There are two types of toners commonly in use for black and white print finishing. By all means, you don't have to tone your finished print, but it can help to add depth to the shadows. Selenium and sepia are the two you'll run into. I'd say that with the current trend in sepia toned filters that you already know that sepia ranges from deep brown to gold. Selenium has more of a purple blue tone to it.

If you do choose to tone your images, you should know that there is some benefit to it. The selenium in particular acts as a protectant and helps make the image more archival. If you want to do this, all you have to do is prepare the selenium bath and dip it in. This won't affect your shadows or highlights at all.

Selenium is also good for just slightly making shadows deeper and richer. It also cools the photo perceptibly.

Sepia is a warming toner, and can range from very subtle yellow in the highlights to a deep brown overall.

Experiment with different times for soaking the print, and different concentrations of the toner to get different results. Label the back of your prints and keep a record of them to refer back to later.

Final Print Preparation

By this point, your prints are probably hanging out in the water bath. As I stated in the chapter on making prints, it's best to let them wash in moving water for 20–30 minutes. Next, you're going to put them in a tray with enough paper fixer remover to cover them, and for the next 5–10 minutes, you need to shuffle the prints through the chemistry. This will remove any excess chemistry that might still be caught in the paper, and the shuffling keeps fresh chemistry moving over the paper so that it doesn't become exhausted.

After you're done with the fixer remover, it's time to put your images in the archival wash. You should leave the prints there for at least 20 minutes, though you can leave them up to an hour. I wouldn't suggest any longer than that though, because otherwise the emulsion can begin to peel away from the paper.

When you get them out, they have to be squeegeed to remove the excess water, otherwise they'll never dry, and will be more susceptible to rack marks. Do the front and the back, and be firm but gentle. The last thing you want is to rip a finished print, and believe me, it happens.

Finally, you want to put your images on a drying rack. Make sure they're spaced out enough to not touch, because they will stick together and rip. Some people like to dry their images face up to avoid rack marks, but again, if they've been wrung out enough, this shouldn't really be an issue. I don't like to dry images face up because if there are images on the rack above, you get water drips on your images. You also get a lot of dust, which is a pain in the neck to remove.

Leave your images there at least for the night. In the morning they'll have to be heat pressed to remove the curling. If you are using a traditional heat press, you can stick the prints directly into the press, although if you're worried about burning you can always place them, stacked, in between two pieces of cardboard. Alternatively, if you don't have access to a heat press, you can use a dry iron with cardboard over the image to protect it. I find that it takes about two minutes to press about five images altogether.

Your prints are now ready for matting and framing.

Making Scans and Developing Digitally

Some people like to make direct scans of the images they've made, and while that's fine and it works, I find that scanning the film produces a better quality image. I learned how to scan on an Imacon scanner, but those are very expensive and unless you go to school for photography or have the extreme luck to have access to a studio that has one, you'll probably have to use a flatbed scanner. That works just fine, but if you're buying one of your own, I would suggest an Epson flatbed that's made for film so that you also get the film scanning kit with it. The film scanning kit comes with a 4x5, 120mm, and 35mm magnetic holder that makes it much easier to hold the film still.

Every scanner is different, so I'll just provide some generalized guidelines for the Imacon and general flatbed scanners.

First things first, when you scan, you should come prepared with gloves, canned air, and an anti-static cloth. Wipe down your work area and spray it off to get rid of as much dust as you can beforehand. This leads to less cleanup in post. Make sure your film strip lines up with the magnetized holder, otherwise the scan will be off. Clipping it in can be finicky, so just do it again if the Imacon doesn't want to cooperate. Go into the Flextight program and open it up. The first thing you want to do to prep is to turn off the sharpening on the image. Then you need to select the type of film that you have and the ISO from the dropdown menu. In this case, you want to make sure that the type you select also reads negative, otherwise the machine thinks your negative is a positive. Then set your ppi to a high resolution, especially if you want to print them large later. Be careful though; if you change your format or film type, the resolution also resets to 300, so just be sure to double check things before you hit scan. You should see a preview, then you'll be asked to name your final scan.

So that's all the technical, but what about edits? Many people, when they first learn to scan, mistakenly believe that you should edit your photo to look like you want the finished product to. But I'm here to tell you that this scan is like your master copy, your RAW file, and your job here is not to make it look aesthetically pleasing, but to capture as much information from the film as you can. This often means tamping down highlights that you really want to be brighter, and lifting shadows you want to be deep and dark. Make sure you can see every detail of the image, and that you're as close to a proper exposure as is possible. Generally, one film strip is going to be fairly similar in exposure so you should be able to make generalized corrections to the entire strip. However, if you do find that you have an outlier or that the photos need some individual tweaking, you can select it and only edit that picture.

The end result of this process is going to look very grey and unappealing, but I promise you it will give you the best image to edit in Photoshop or Lightroom.

If you have to use a flatbed scanner, just make sure that you have a way to secure the negatives if you don't have the film holders, and make sure that it's set on Professional mode at a reasonably high ppi. I would say at least 600.

Now, you can bring your scans into Photoshop and clean them up. If you haven't made darkroom prints yet, I would suggest doing this part first, especially if you plan on using advanced darkroom techniques. This way, you can experiment without wasting paper. Figure out what aesthetic you want and do it on the digital copy. Take notes for what you would have to do to get it to correspond in the darkroom. It will make your life much easier.

Conclusion

It is my hope that you are now more confident in the art of darkroom photography. If this is a brand new foray for you, hopefully you are more excited than overwhelmed, and curious about stepping into a darkroom. Now you know how to set up your own darkroom, and make a photograph from start to finish.

Once you've mastered the basics of how to develop your film, begin to experiment with the contrast to see if you find a style you like better. The same goes for the actual prints. Once you've learned how to make a good, solid, basic print on glossy paper, begin to experiment with the dodging and burning techniques I go through in chapter 8. Learn to fully express yourself through your prints and find all the possibilities you can in your images.

Learning analog can be a frustrating and long journey, but if you're truly passionate or curious about learning it, make sure you stick with it, because it's very rewarding. Even if you find that it's not your thing, I hope that you will at least learn the basics. I say this because doing analog makes you much more meticulous. Mistakes are much harder to correct, so it's better to get it right with each step you take. And the more careful you are, the better quality your final image will be. Even if you go back to digital completely, you'll find that your work gets much stronger after learning some darkroom skills. This is because you learn to be much more meticulous about each step you take, and thus have a higher standard of quality for yourself. You also end up having less work to do in post.

So as you begin your journey, take your time, be patient with yourself, be willing to experiment and make mistakes, and have fun.

www.ingramcontent.com/pod-product-compliance
Lightning Source LLC
Chambersburg PA
CBHW070230210526
45168CB00019B/1663